# WHAT IS VIRTUAL REAL[ITY]

## Contents

Written by Imogen Mellor

## Collins

## What is virtual reality?

Virtual reality, or VR, is a technology that allows **software developers** to let you see something that isn't really there. Virtual images look like you can reach out and touch them, but they're on a screen.

# How does VR work?

Your eyes and your brain are very clever. Two eyes allow you to see slightly different versions of objects in front of you. Close one eye at a time and see the difference! Small differences in each eye tells your brain that there is something in front of you that you can touch.

VR does the same thing. Two small screens, one for each eye, show you objects from slightly different angles, so your brain thinks those virtual objects are **3D**. If you've seen a 3D film in the cinema, those special glasses help the same thing to happen!

## What can VR be used for?

Many things! The most common use of VR is in video games. Games are made to tell incredible stories and it can be more exciting if you feel like you're in the game's world too. You could fly a spaceship, dive underwater, walk on the moon and more, with VR's help.

In some games, you can even take a mini holiday. You can play with silly robots or chill out by the pool, as though you really are on a summer holiday. All you need is some real ice-cream.

VR can also be used for education. Teachers can show students sights all around the world, from the Egyptian pyramids to the Great Barrier Reef. VR can be used for anything you want your own eyes to see.

You can even use VR to control a drone.

## What things do you need for VR?

To see VR, you normally need very special goggles you wear on your head and over your eyes. Inside the goggles are two small screens showing the wearer a virtual reality. However, some big **smartphones** can be used for VR if they're put inside certain special goggles too. This way the phone, when it's very close to your face, can show you two images just like the special VR goggles do.

VR goggles

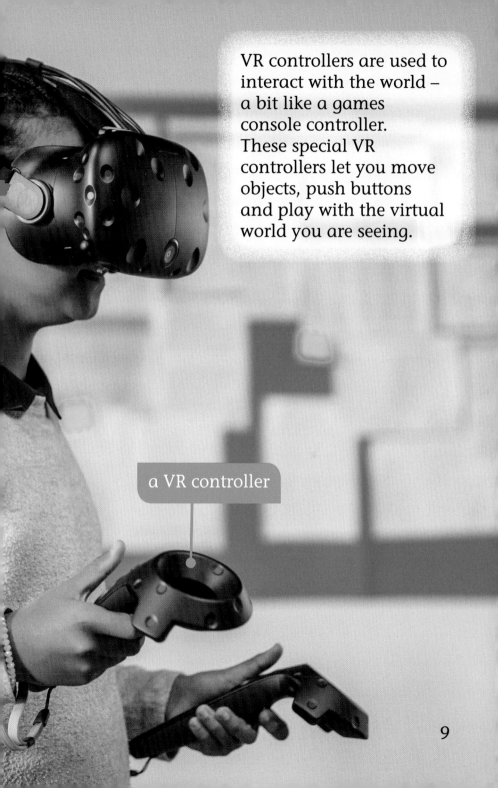

VR controllers are used to interact with the world – a bit like a games console controller. These special VR controllers let you move objects, push buttons and play with the virtual world you are seeing.

a VR controller

## Do I need a special VR room?

You don't need a special room, but you do need space! When using VR, you can't see the real world around you so it's important to have plenty of space so that you don't hurt yourself, or anyone else. Sometimes people forget they're in a virtual world, so they try to reach out and grab objects that aren't really there! It looks very funny to anyone watching them.

There aren't many VR places you can go and use VR goggles, but this might change in the future as more people use them. When you're older, you may be able to buy VR goggles of your own.

**Will I use VR in the future?**

Yes! VR is going to be even more popular in the future. Today it's used for games, but tomorrow it could be used to see what astronauts experience on the moon, or to travel around the world, all from your own home.

You might even meet dinosaurs with VR when the technology is ready.

One day, you might even have gloves to let you interact with the VR in front of you.

# What is augmented reality?

Augmented reality, or AR, is the way you see your world, but just a little different. AR uses the world around you to show you how real or even fantasy objects might look if they were right next to you.

A clever camera that uses AR can work out how, for example, a bear might look in your room. It sees your floor space and uses maths to work out how big that bear might look in your room and puts it on the screen.

# What's the difference between AR and VR?

Augmented reality and virtual reality allow you to see virtual objects. But VR is an entirely virtual world (it's not real), whereas AR shows you the real world with things added.

If you played a game like Pokémon GO using VR, this is what you would see on the screen. The Pokémon isn't real, and the background doesn't look real.

If you played Pokémon GO using AR, however, this is what you would see on the screen. The Pokémon isn't real, but the background is real, so it looks like the Pokémon is actually there, standing in front of you.

## What can you use AR for?

Like VR, AR can be used in video games. This game uses real cards. With the help of AR, you can see extra content through the screen.

AR is a fun way to interact with fictional creatures and objects. Showing you the size of a big German Shepherd compared to a tiny sausage dog is something possible using AR technology. Sadly, you can't pet them through the screen!

AR can also be used for education, like VR. If you look at the ruins of an old castle, AR on a screen could show you what the castle looked like when it was still standing. It lets you have a peek back at hundreds of years of exciting history.

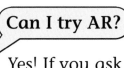

**Can I try AR?**

Yes! If you ask an adult for help, you can see funny AR uses on a mobile phone. By using apps, you can make yourself look like a dog or a cat, give your face a funny shape, and even change your hair to any colour of the rainbow!

So, that's what virtual reality is.

## Glossary

**3D** three-dimensional, so you can see an object's height, width and depth

**smartphones** mobile phones you can connect to the internet

**software developers** people who write computer code

## Index

# Gadgets

VR goggles

smartphone

controller

# What you can do

control a drone

see the world

meet dinosaurs

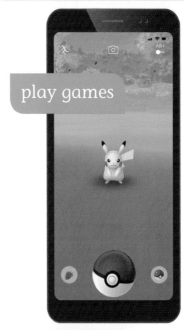

play games

visit space

# Ideas for reading

Written by Christine Whitney
*Primary Literacy Consultant*

**Reading objectives:**
- discuss how items of information are related
- be introduced to non-fiction books that are structured in different ways
- explain and discuss their understanding of books

**Spoken language objectives:**
- ask relevant questions
- speculate, imagine and explore ideas through talk
- participate in discussions

**Curriculum links:** Computing: Recognise common uses of information technology; Writing: Write for different purposes

**Word count:** 1004

**Interest words:** virtual reality, augmented reality, 3D

**Resources:** paper, pencils and crayons, a range of children's books that use augmented reality

## Build a context for reading

- Ask children if they have ever seen a 3D film. Support their understanding of 3D.
- Read the title of the book and ask children to discuss what they think virtual reality is. Do they have any experience of this?
- Encourage children to name three things about virtual reality they would like to know. Keep these questions and see if they are answered by reading the book.

## Understand and apply reading strategies

- Read up to page 5 together and ask children to explain to each other what they understand about how VR works.
- Continue to read to page 11. Ask children why a large space is needed when using VR.
- On page 14, it says, *A clever camera that uses AR can work out how, for example, a bear might look in your room.* How does it do this?